SQUADRONS!

No. 7

THE SUPERMARINE
SPITFIRE F. 21

Phil H. Listemann

ISBN: 978-2918590-46-0

Copyright

© 2014 Philedition - Phil Listemann
Revised - Feb.2019, Mar.2021

Colour profiles: Gaetan Marie/Bravo Bravo Aviation

All right reserved. No part of this book may be reproduced, stored in a retrieval system or transmitted in any form by any means, electronic, mechanical, photocopying, recording or otherwise, without prior permission of the author.

Glossary of Terms

Personel :

(AUS)/RAF: Australian serving in the RAF
(BEL)/RAF: Belgian serving in the RAF
(CAN)/RAF: Canadian serving in the RAF
(CZ)/RAF: Czechoslovak serving in the RAF
(NFL)/RAF: Newfoundlander serving in the RAF
(NL)/RAF: Dutch serving in the RAF
(NZ)/RAF: New Zealander serving in the RAF
(POL)/RAF: Pole serving in the RAF
(RHO)/RAF: Rhodesian serving in the RAF
(SA)/RAF: South African serving in the RAF
(US)/RAF - RCAF : American serving in the RAF or RCAF

Ranks

G/C : Group Captain
W/C : Wing Commander
S/L : Squadron Leader
F/L : Flight Lieutenant
F/O : Flying Officer
P/O : Pilot Officer
W/O : Warrant Officer
F/Sgt : Flight Sergeant
Sgt : Sergeant
Cpl : Corporal
LAC : Leading Aircraftman

Other

ATA: Air Transport Auxiliary
CO : Commander
DFC : Distinguished Flying Cross
DFM : Distinguished Flying Medal
DSO : Distinguished Service Order
Eva. : Evaded
ORB : Operational Record Book
OTU : Operational Training Unit
PoW : Prisoner of War
PAF: Polish Air Force
RAF : Royal Air Force
RAAF : Royal Australian Air Force
RCAF : Royal Canadian Air Force
RNZAF : Royal New Zealand Air Force
SAAF : South African Air Force
s/d: Shot down
Sqn : Squadron
† : Killed

Codenames - Offensive Operations - Fighter Command

Circus:
Bombers heavily escorted by fighters, the purpose being to bring enemy fighters into combat.

Ramrod:
Bombers escorted by fighters, the primary aim being to destroy a target.

Ranger:
Large formation freelance intrusion over enemy territory with aim of wearing down enemy figthers.

Rhubard:
Freelance fighter sortie against targets of opportunity.

Rodeo:
A fighter sweep without bombers.

Sweep:
An offensive flight by fighters designed to draw up and clear the enemy from the sky.

The Spitfire F. XXI (F. 21)

The Spitfire F.21 was the first model of the last generation of Spitfires and the second powered by a Griffon engine. A new wing was designed to improve performance. It eventually replaced the one designed by Reginald Mitchell that was, until then, fitted to all previous marks. Indeed, the original design of the Spitfire had reached its limits and, to be able to use more powerful engines, it had been necessary to rethink the whole structure. While the overall look remained the same, as far as we are talking about what the airframe had inside, it was almost a totally new aircraft. Changes made this new design more robust and, compared to the Mk. XIV, the new Spitfire was more slender. The ailerons were also enlarged and, as they were now all metal (instead of fabric-covered), they were able to absorb greater loading factors. The engine remained the Griffon already used on earlier marks but the version chosen, the R-R 61, was a bit different from the 65 used in the Spitfire XIV even though it had the same power rating. A five-blade propeller, as used on the F.XIV Spitfire, absorbed this power.

The fuel system was completely revised (and therefore more complicated!) and required finer fuel management from the pilot. Standard armament was now four Hispano 20 mm cannon which gave very respectable firepower. It was a big step forward compared to previous marks. These changes were such that Supermarine initially though about changing the aircraft's name to 'Victor', probably thinking that this aircraft would be in service in numbers on the day of victory, but the reality was to be different in May 1945. In any case, this never occurred and the legend of Spitfire was able to continue for a while longer. Compared to the Spitfire F.XIV, the F.21 had a similar performance but it was heavier (an increase of more than 8% of the empty weight and over 16% of normal loaded weight). This could be achieved thanks to the new wing. The first real prototype Spitfire F.21 (PP139) first flew on 24 July, 1943.

This new generation, showing great promise, was then logically chosen to replace all existing fighters then in service and the Air Ministry was quick to order the F.21 in numbers. A first contract for 1,500 aircraft, to be built by the Castle Bromwich plant, was signed on 6 June, 1943. Another order of 700 machines followed on 20 January, 1944, and 800 more twelve days later. Again it was Castle Bromwich that took charge of manufacturing. Because of various delays, in part due to problems with longitudinal stability, these contracts were either cancelled or amended in August 1944 in favour of the Spitfire F.IX which was a mark no longer seen as the best mark but available immediately. However, later on, a contract of cancelled Spitfire Mk Vs was reactivated leading to the production of 120 Spitfire F.21s - **LA187-LA236** (50), **LA249-284** (36), **LA299-LA332** (34). This order was placed awaiting the arrival of the Spitfire F.22 as the F.21 was now only seen as an interim mark. The first production aircraft, LA187, made its maiden flight on 27 January 1944 and the last F.21s built flew in December 1945. The 120th and final Spitfire F.21, LA332, was finally delivered to the RAF on 2 January, 1946. Even though built in small numbers, the F.21 was the last Spitfire mark to be put into service before the war ended. Deliveries began in July 1944 but remained slow at first. Thirty-three Spitfires had flown by 31 December, 1944, but only 18 were actually taken on charge by the RAF. This was not enough to convert a single fighter squadron at that time. The other F.21s were used for various tests either by the manufacturer or by the A&AEE. On VE-Day, 38 more F.21s had flown and 34 additional machines made available for the RAF making conversion of operational squadrons possible by the eve of spring 1945.

Those delays were caused by several issues. The prototype was briefly tested at Boscombe Down but the initial report was unflattering as stability problems were noted and changes requested. The recommendations were severe, especially regarding yaw instability, and required the grounding of the aircraft until a solution was found. The plane was not unsafe to fly as such but the concerns were about what could happen in the hands of average pilots and many accidents were therefore expected. The work required to be carried out was rather simple but required several months to complete. As it had been decided to start the production of the Spitfire F.21, it was imperative to ensure the flight characteristics of the F.21 would be tolerable enough for an average pilot. It was expected the new Spitfire's successor, the F.22, would overcome these shortcomings. It took three months to make the necessary changes. In March 1945, pilots of the AFDU (Air Fighting Development Unit) found a significant improvement in the stability of a modified F.21 - LA215 - and recommended that all machines already built undergo the same modifications. The Spitfire F.21 was then officially declared combat ready but was to have a rather short career in the regular RAF squadrons although it did last a bit longer in

The prototype Spitfire F.XXI (later designated F.21) PP139 received the nickname 'Victor'. This denomination was eventually dropped on 1 November 1943. It is worth noting that this serial had also been allocated to a Short Sunderland. PP139 was the second airframe to be designated as a Mark 21, after DP851, but PP139 was the true prototype of this mark.

Above, LA187, first production F.21, prior to completion to full F.21 standard. It was used for various tests and was never issued to any squadron.

the Auxiliary squadrons. The type was declared obsolete by May 1953. About 80 F.21s were used by the RAF or the RAuxAF. Fifteen never saw any kind of service and a further 15 were used by the manufacturer for various tests. Some aircraft were fitted with a contra-rotating prop built by Rotol. Rotol supplied a number of experimental propellers for the F.21 production aircraft in an attempt to select the best possible variant for the various Griffon engines available but none would be actually accepted.

Below, LA191 was also used for various tests at A&AEE and RAE and was eventually allocated to No. 615 Sqn, late in the career of the F.21, in April 1947. It was struck off charge the following December.

Test flown in December 1944, LA215 would be issued to No. 91 Squadron as DL-T in March 1945 and then after the war with No. 615 Squadron as RAV-A

January 1945
October 1946

Victories - confirmed or probable claims: -

First operational sortie:
10.04.45
Last operational sortie:
01.05.45

Number of sorties: 154
Total aircraft written-off: 5

Aircraft lost on operations: 2
Aircraft lost in accidents: 3

Squadron code letters:
DL

COMMANDING OFFICERS

S/L Peter McC. Bond	RAF No. 40073	RAF	...	01.03.45
S/L Irvine P.J. Maskill	NZ41487	RNZAF	01.03.45	18.01.46
S/L David E. Proudlove	RAF No. 111108	RAF	20.03.46	03.04.46
S/L Archibald R. Hall	RAF No. 87453	RAF	20.03.46	03.04.46
S/L Clifford K. Gray	RAF No. 81370	RAF	01.04.46	...

SQUADRON USAGE

Squadron Leader Irvine Maskill was the pilot who led No. 91 Sqn in combat during the last days of the war. A New Zealander, he had served with No. 485 (NZ) Sqn for his first tour in 1942-1943 with which he made his only claim, a Bf109 in March 1942. He served with Nos. 1 and 91 Sqn for his second tour. During his command, he was awarded the DFC in April 1945 for his actions with No.1 Sqn.

The Spitfire F.21 was ready for combat. The RAF selected No. 91 "Nigeria" Squadron to be the first operational unit. The squadron was one of the most experienced Spitfire units and had had the privilege to fly the Spitfire Mk.XII, one of only two units to have flown this mark on operations, and then the Mk.XIV before switching to an older mark, the IX, while under 2TAF authority. The Squadron, now based at Manston, was commanded by Peter Bond who had been flying with 91 as a supernumerary Squadron Leader for a year and had taken command of the squadron in August when the previous CO, S/L Kynaston, had been killed in action. The squadron received its first two Spitfire F.21s, LA210 and LA212, on 4 January. Other F.21s followed during the month (LA196, LA203 & LA207 on 7 January, LA205 on the 18th) but training was slow to start as the squadron continued to carry out operational sorties on Mk IXs. The pilots were delighted with their new mount. It is interesting to note that the pilots still had unmodified machines meaning that the problems associated with the early aircraft were perhaps not as severe and were of more concern to the engineers and test pilots than for the pilots of 91 who, by sheer flying skill, were able to 'fix' the problems!

In February and March, other Mk.21s were taken on charge - LA208 on 22 February, LA221 on 24 February, LA197, LA225 & LA226 on 7 March, LA224 & LA234 on 9 March, LA223 on 13 March and, on 23 March, LA235 & LA236. However, the pilots were rather disappointed as they were not authorised to fly over enemy lines (probably to prevent this latest version of the Spitfire falling prematurely into the hands of the Germans). In March, training continued on the Mk XXI (F.21) and operations continued with the Mk.IX under the command of a new CO, Squadron-Leader Irvine Maskill, a young New Zealander aged 25, posted from No.1 Squadron where he had been serving as a Flight Commander. By April, 91 was ready to start operations on the F.21. On 4 April, 1945, the Squadron carried out its last mission on Spitfire Mk IXs. On 8 April, the Squadron moved to Ludham in Norfolk to play a more offensive role, only taking the F.21s (18 of which had now been allocated to the unit). The new tasks assigned to 91 were the attack of Dutch targets, V-2 sites and the destruction of midget submarines. This is an area of operations that especially pleased the only Dutch pilot on the

Spitfire F.21 LA200 seen at dispersal at Ludham in April 1945. It was the regular mount of F/L Arthur Elcock, a V-1 ace. He was killed shortly after VE-Day flying LA203. LA200 was lost two days earlier with another pilot at the controls.

squadron, Flight Lieutenant van L. Eendenburg. However, it must be noted that these tasks were far from the air superiority role for which the Spitfire F.21 had been designed. Furthermore, as the last V-2 was soon launched against Britain, destroying V-2 sites quickly became unnecessary.

On 10 April, the first F.21 operational sortie was carried out. Two aircraft took off at 7:30 am to undertake an armed reconnaissance over Holland. They were flown by Flight Lieutenant H.D. Johnson (LA236) and Flying Officer J.A. Faulkner (LA221). They returned to base at 9:10 without having anything to report. The day wasn't over for 91 as three more missions were flown during the day (9:40,

LA223 was issued to No. 91 Sqn in March 1945 and left in September. It was re-issued again in July 1947 to No. 602 Sqn. LA223 made a forced landing one year later, putting an end to its career with the RAF.

Summary of the aircraft lost on Operations - 91 Squadron

Date	Pilot	S/N	Origin	Serial	Code	Fate
10.04.45	F/L Roy A. Cruickshank	Can./ J.11143	RCAF	**LA234**	DL-V	-
	F/O John A. Faulkner	Can./ J.27233	RCAF	**LA229**		-

Total: 2

10:35 and 7:10 p.m.). Each comprised four aircraft except for the last which consisted of a single section of two Spitfires. During the second mission, at 9:40, Flight Lieutenant A.R. Cruicksbank and Flying Officer Faulkner (both RCAF) attacked boats off the port of Den Helder on their return flight. Both pilots probably underestimated the danger as within a couple of seconds they were under fire from particularly intense flak and both aircraft were promptly shot down. They both survived and were recovered later by an ASR mission. No one could say that it was a particularly great start for the F.21's war with two losses for no return! Generally speaking, only one month before the end of war in Europe, the enemy air activity was low and the F.21s had to make do by continuing to carry out anti-submarine patrols and armed reconnaissance. Of course, the pilots did their job but they had one wish - to fly against German fighters. The squadron flew every day except on 14 April when the weather was too bad. On the 13th, the Squadron carried out 24 anti-submarine patrols and, despite all this effort, nothing was reported on return to base. On 26 April, Flight Lieutenant W.P. Draper (RCAF) accompanied by Flight Lieutenant W.C. Marshall spotted a class " Biber " midget submarine, cruising at about 300 m off the Dutch coast, and wasted no time in attacking. Both aircraft dived from 1,000 feet to 50 feet and opened fire, obtaining strikes on the superstructure around the conning tower, which brought the submarine almost to a standstill. The section made a second attack from a northerly direction but from the same height. Strikes were again scored and the submarine was seen to sink and left a large patch of oil on the surface. Both pilots fired a short burst at the oil patch and headed to base where they claimed the 'Biber' submarine as destroyed. On 1 May, 1945, two Spitfires piloted by Flight Lieutenant A. Smith and Pilot Officer L.A. King (LA206 and LA197 respectively) took off at 9:35 for another anti-submarine mission. They returned to base at 10:40 because of the rather poor weather. They did not know it yet but the war was over for the Spitfire F.21 after just 154 operational sorties.

VE-Day was soon proclaimed, duly celebrated and no flights were flown over the next few days. The pilots experienced the rapid change from the wartime operating they were so familiar with to new peacetime flying rules. Some adjustment was necessary! Flights now consisted only of navigation or aerobatics sessions. It was during one of these that Flying Officer Geoff Kay was killed on 12 May. Kay became the first pilot to be killed in a Spitfire F.21 but, two days later, he was sadly joined by Flight Lieutenant Arthur Elcock who was killed when he crashed on landing just 100 yards from where Kay had died. No.91 Squadron continued to fly the Spitfire F.21 until late 1946. In June 1945, the number of hours flown remained significant with more than 330 flight hours completed for the month but a year later the flying hours had fallen to only about one hundred hours. The squadron kept its Spitfires until October 1946 when it converted to the jet age with the Meteor F.3. During that period of time, one more F.21 was wrecked. The fateful day was 25 January, 1946. The aircraft stalled on landing and the starboard wing dropped and dug into the ground. The aircraft tipped onto its nose and skidded along before the undercarriage collapsed.

Summary of the aircraft lost by accident - 91 Squadron

Date	Pilot	S/N	Origin	Serial	Code	Fate
12.05.45	F/O Geoffrey Kay	RAF No. 182604	RAF	**LA200**	DL-E	†
14.05.45	F/L Arthur R. Elcock	RAF No. 125505	RAF	**LA203**		†
25.01.46	W/O Thomas Mutch	RAF No. 1567244	RAF	**LA266**		-

Total: 3

Line-up of No. 91 Squadron's Spitfire 21s at Lubeck (Germany) during summer 1946. LA279 (DL-U), LA205 (DL-F) and LA265 (DL-K) can be seen. All later served with auxiliary squadrons.

With the Other Regular RAF Units

When the war ended it was intended that the Spitfire F.21 would equip other units. The next squadron on the list was No. 1 Squadron which was flying the Spitfire Mk IX. The first F.21 (LA201) was issued on 1 February, 1945, but re-equipment was very slow as, three months later, only a handful of aircraft had been delivered to the squadron. It was not until 8 May that the normal planned allocation was reached but the war in Europe was over. As for No. 91 Squadron, No. 1 kept its F.21s until October 1946. No. 1 Squadron lost two aircraft during this period. The first accident occurred on 27 September, 1945, when LA303 suffered an engine failure shortly after take-off. The pilot, F/O Thomas Glaser, tried to return to Hawkinge where the squadron was based but, in stretching the glide, the aircraft eventually stalled when it was at low altitude leaving no chance for the pilot to recover. The Spitfire crashed with its pilot near the eastern end of the runway and was destroyed in the subsequent fire. It seems that Glaser was killed in the impact and not by the fire. The second accident occurred a couple of months later, on 1 April, but this time without major consequences for the pilot. On final approach at Hutton Cranswick, where No.1 Squadron had been relocated since October 1945, the flaps of LA219 retracted and the aircraft landed flapless and, of course, too fast. It overshot the runway and was so heavily damaged it was declared damaged beyond economic repair later on. As for 91, No.1 Squadron gave up its F.21s for the Meteor F.3.

No.1 Sqn was the second RAF squadron to be converted to the F.21. LA267 was issued on 30 September, 1945, and ended its career with No. 602 Sqn at the end of the forties. *(Andrew Thomas)*

Summary of the aircraft lost by accident - 1 Squadron

Date	Pilot	S/N	Origin	Serial	Code	Fate
27.09.45	F/O Thomas **Glaser**	RAF No. 188989	RAF	**LA303**		†
01.04.46	W/O Alec H. **Ross**	RAF No. 1621009	RAF	**LA219**	JX-3	-

Total: 2

Group shot of members of No. 1 Sqn after its arrival at Tangmere in 1946. A few Spitfire F.21s can be identified – LA273/JX-D, LA275/JX-E on the right and LA201/JX-S on the left, the latter having the serial repeated in white above the fin flash. LA227 in the foreground also has the serial repeated above the fin flash but painted in black. Note the Spitfire in the background, Mk IX MK515/JX-N, used as hack by the squadron.
(Andrew Thomas collection)

A rare view of a Spitfire of No. 122 Sqn. Behind, a Spitfire F.21 of No. 41 Sqn can be seen. It is possible that this photo was taken shortly after 122 was re-numbered in April 1946, the aircraft still in the process of having the squadron codes changed from MT to EB (the Spitfire just behind carrying the letters EB).

The number of squadrons equipped with the Spitfire F.21 was limited to two in 1945 but, in 1946, a third was added, No.122 Squadron. Re-equipped with Mk.IXs in August 1945, 122 switched to the F.21 in February 1946 but two months later it was renumbered No. 41 Squadron. Despite this short period of time, the squadron lost one pilot who was killed. This occurred on 8 March after an engine failure at 4,000 feet while flying over the sea 3 miles north of Lossiemouth. It is believed that Flight Lieutenant A. Sutherland – who had been awarded the DFC the previous August for his service with 111 Squadron - tried to bale out at 700 feet but unfortunately he probably drowned because he was not wearing a lifejacket - his aircraft was equipped with a dinghy though - and his body was never recovered. Consequently No. 41 Squadron became the last regular unit to use the Spitfire F.21 so, in the middle of 1946, the RAF had three squadrons flying this mark. It was, however, only for a short time as, in October that year, Nos. 1 and 91 transitioned to the Meteor, and left 41 to go on flying its F.21s. This situation remained until August 1947 when the squadron began its conversion to the de Havilland Hornet F.1. No. 41 Squadron lost three Spitfire F.21s, one on 23 April 1946 and two in November the same year (15th and 22nd). Fortunately there was no loss of life. It is worth noting that the three aircraft were lost on landing. Many causes can be found for this but the main one is probably the low number of hours flown by the fighter pilots in 1946-1947. It was sometimes simply not enough to keep a good level of proficiency with a powerful aircraft like the Spitfire F.21. As with any aircraft, stalling the F.21 was a dangerous situation to be avoided.

Summary of the aircraft lost by accident - 122 Squadron

Date	Pilot	S/N	Origin	Serial	Code	Fate
08.03.46	F/O Alexander SUTHERLAND	RAF No. 174225	RAF	**LA251**		†

Total: 1

Summary of the aircraft lost by accident - 41 Squadron

Date	Pilot	S/N	Origin	Serial	Code	Fate
23.04.46	F/Sgt Thomas L.P. DELANEY	RAF No. 1806853	RAF	**LA282**		-
15.11.46	F/L Lionel H. DAWES	RAF No. 112699	RAF	**LA302**		-
22.11.46	W/O Charles RUSSELL	RAF No. 1551495	RAF	**LA284**		-

Above, view of No. 41 Squadron's Spitfire F.21s, shortly it was renumbered from No. 122 Squadron in April 1946, while based at Dalcross in UK.
Below, LA315 has the individual letter 'O', something unusual in RAF squadrons but could be explained by the fact that the aircraft was also flown by the Wittering Station Flight.

Several photos showing various No. 41 Squadron Spitfire F.21s during summer 1946. At that time, 41 Sqn had moved to Lubeck for a couple of weeks as part of the occupation forces in Germany. *(41 Squadron Archive)*

Loaded with small exercise bombs under the belly, two No. 1 Squadron Spitfire taxi for their next take-off from Lubeck in Germany. Note the large size of the serial number under the wings the aircraft leading (LA225). *(41 Squadron Archive)*

With the RAuxAF and other units

In August 1947, the Spitfire F.21 ended its career as a frontline fighter. However, its career under British markings continued for a while with the creation of the Auxiliary Air Force in June 1946. The RAuxAF, as it was named in December 1946 with the addition of the prefix "Royal", had, as its first task, to provide practice to the pilots of the RAF held in Reserve. At that time, most of these pilots had already seen combat during the war. Three squadrons were partially equipped with the F.21, No.600 Squadron "City of London", No. 602 Squadron "City of Glasgow" and No. 615 Squadron "County of Surrey". These units began to receive their new mount in January 1947 and by spring the three units were flying this model. Later on, some F.22s were added to the inventory and these flew alongside the F.21s. These three RAuxAF units reported a couple of accidents up to November 1950 when the last F.21 was withdrawn from the RAuxAF. In all, ten machines were wrecked during this period and two pilots killed. The first was Flying Officer I. Reid, of 602 Squadron, who was killed on 31 July, 1947, during an air-to-air firing sortie. He was seen to make a circle after his engine had failed. The aircraft was then seen to lose height and to crash into the Irish Sea while attempting to ditch. The second pilot to lose his life was Flying Officer H. McWilliam, also from 602 Squadron, on 3 April, 1948. This pilot was rather inexperienced on type and carried out two and half turns of an upward roll before the aircraft entered an inverted spin and crashed into the ground before any recovery action could be taken.

The Spitfire F.21 remained in use with No.3 CAACU until the end of 1953 when the aircraft were placed in storage. Most were scrapped in the following weeks. At that time, half a dozen machines were temporarily saved from the scrappers by being made available to the Burmese Converting Squadron (BCS) operating with the Central Flying School. This unit was created to allow Burmese pilots to undergo training on Spitfires powered by Griffon engines. The Spitfire F.21s made available or this task were LA231, LA236, LA253, LA316, LA325 and LA331. Burma had already bought, in the early fifties, 20 Seafire F.15s stripped of their naval equipment. However, as the training had proved more difficult than expected in Burma, a group of pilots had been sent to Britain to complete the training. This training was successful but at the cost of two aircraft. On 4 December, 1952, Pilot Officer Au Min seriously damaged LA253 on taking off. He raised the tail too early on the take-off run and the propeller struck the runway. The Spitfire overturned instantly. The pilot miraculously emerged from the wreckage unscathed. His compatriot, Pilot Officer Sein Hla Maung, survived a similar adventure a couple of weeks later but this time on landing at Llandow. The pilot lost control as the aircraft was touched the ground and, drifting to starboard, the undercarriage collapsed. The Spitfire was not repaired.

During the F.21's post-war career, other accidents occurred involving miscellaneous units and in all 28 F.21s were struck off charge following accidents. Of these, one was fatal for its pilot and occurred on 18 February, 1946. The pilot was Flight Lieutenant E.G. Filmore flying LA216 (which was used by Rotol Ltd at that time). The aircraft crashed in bad weather while it was on an endurance trial fitted with a contra-rotating propeller. Filmore was a former WW2 Lancaster pilot and had been awarded the DFC in 1944. Also, other F.21s were used by various Station Flights or schools – CFS or HCCS - and were generally reserved as the personal mounts of high-ranking officers.

Based logically at Biggin Hill, No. 600 Sqn 'City of London' of the RAuxAF converted to the F.21 in July 1946. The F.21 remained the main equipment until some F.22s were taken on charge in 1948. The RAuxAF squadron codes allocated to 600 Sqn were RAG. Note the blue spinner of an aircraft from No. 615 Sqn (also an RAuxAF unit).

In 1954 it was the end of the road for the Spitfire F.21., Most of the remaining aircraft left for the scrapyard and others found further use by becoming instructional airframes. The final two machines on strength, LA208 and LA312, were struck from the inventory on 1 October, 1954. Ordered as an interim aircraft pending deliveries of the F.22, the F.21's career, while mostly in peacetime, lasted almost a decade. Not too bad!

Summary of the aircraft lost by accident - RAuxAF

Date	Pilot	S/N	Origin	Serial	Code	Unit	Fate
31.07.47	F/O Robert I. **Reid**	RAuxAF No. 91253	RAuxAF	**LA211**	RAI-K	602 Sqn	†
03.04.48	F/O Hamish **McWilliam**	RAF No. 163749	RAF	**LA268**	RAI-H	602 Sqn	-
03.06.48	F/L Michael W. **Grierson Jackson**	RAF No. 67092	RAF	**LA193**	RAI-E	602 Sqn	-
28.08.48	F/L Archibald W. **Robinson**	RAuxAF No. 91256	RAuxAF	**LA279**	RAI-J	602 Sqn	-
31.10.48	P.2 James A. **Johnston**	RAF No. 2683046	RAF	**LA222**	RAI-M	602 Sqn	-
08.05.49	P/O John McR. **Cormack**	RAF No. 193473	RAF	**LA330**	RAG-F	600 Sqn	-
18.06.49	P/O John A. **Forrest**	RAF No. 187680	RAF	**LA275**	RAI-H	602 Sqn	-
18.06.49	P/O Richard T.G. **Williams**	RAF No. 197717	RAF	**LA323**	RAG-H	600 Sqn	-
04.05.50	P.2 Frank **Scott**	RAF No. 2685039	RAF	**LA329**		602 Sqn	-

Some more photos of F.21s of the RAuxAF. LA228 of No. 600 Sqn, left in natural metal finish, and LA192 and LA253 flying in formation in 1948.

LA275/RAI-H of No. 602 Sqn 'City of Glasgow' based at Abbottsinch (near Glasgow of course). It was lost in an accident in June 1949. Below, another F.21 taken during take-off.

Summary of the aircraft lost by accident - Other Units

Date	Pilot	S/N	Origin	Serial	Code	Unit	Fate
18.02.46	F/L Eric G. Filmore	RAF No. 152845	RAF	**LA216**		Rotol	†
18.12.46	F/O Douglas A. Gardiner	RAF No. 202229	RAF	**LA187**		2. FP	-
23.09.47	F/O Robert B. Connell	RAF No. 184367	RAF	**LA197**		9. MU	-
03.10.49	G/C Edward M. Donaldson	RAF No. 32043	RAF	**LA232**		HCCS	-
01.06.50	F/L Amos J. Rendell	RAF No. 55400	RAF	**LA192**		2. FP	-
30.07.52	Mr Jack W.E. Trill	-	*Civil*	**LA225**		3. CAACU	†
04.12.52	P/O Au Min		BurAF	**LA253**		BCS	-
17.01.53	P/O Sein H. Maung		BurAF	**LA236**		BCS	-
12.02.53	F/L Alec A. Ince	RAF No. 205590	RAF	**LA190**		3. CAACU	-

Two nice views of Spitfire F.21s in flight showing various markings. Above, LA328 of No. 600 Sqn, with a red spinner and letters, while LA195 has the standard Day Fighter Scheme of Fighter Command. No. 615 Sqn flew a mixed fleet of F.21s and F.22s. This squadron returned to Fighter Command authority and changed its codes from RAV to V6. Soon after, 615 relinquished its Spitfires for Meteor F.4s.

A poor quality, but very interesting, photo showing a line-up of Spitfire F.21s of 3 CAACU. The aircraft have had their armament removed. The aircraft that are identifiable are LA280/K and LA304/L.

Spitfire F.21 LA217 served with the Central Fighter Establishment (CFE) in 1946 equipped with a G68 Rotol contra/propeller. It was stored in July 1948 and scrapped in November 1949.

When No. 602 Sqn returned to Fighter Command, the letters switched from RAI of the RAuxAF to the wartime code letters LO. 602 switched to the jet era with the Vampire in 1951 but LA269 was retained as a hack for a little while with this particular paint scheme and markings.

20

LA299, the personal aircraft of the Wittering Station Commander, Group Captain Alfred V. Hammond, with initials 'AVH' and the Group Captain pennant painted on, equipped with a contra-rotating propeller. Born at the turn of the century, he was a pre-war regular RAF officer and held the rank of Squadron Leader at the outbreak of war. He was also known for his paintings.

Another personal aircraft, LA232 coded 'TT' for the initials of Thomas Traill. A former WWI pilot, he was serving in HQ of No. 2 (Bomber) Group when the war broke out and spent the war in various HQ postings in UK and overseas. In May 1946, Thomas C. Traill was posted as acting OC of No. 12 Group of Fighter Command and chose LA232 as his personal mount. This Spitfire F.21 was equipped with a G85 Rotol contra-propeller.

Simplified Register

Serial	month of delivery	Squadron
LA187	Dec.46	-
LA188	Sep.50	-
LA189	Oct.45	-
LA190	Nov.47	**1**
LA191	Feb.46	**615** *(RAV-D)*
LA192	Sep.44	**615** *(RAV-C)*, **600** *(RAG-G)*
LA193	Jan.46	**602**
LA194	Sep.44	**122**
LA195	Jan.46	**615** *(RAV-E)*
LA196	Sep.44	**91, 1, 122, 41**
LA197	Oct.44	**91, 122**
LA198	Oct.44	**1** *(JX-C)*, **602** *(RAI-G)*
LA199	Oct.44	-
LA200	Dec.44	**91** *(DL-E)*
LA201	Nov.44	**1** *(JX-S)*, **91**
LA202	Nov.44	**1** *(JX-Y)*
LA203	Nov.44	**91**
LA204	Nov.44	**91**
LA205	Nov.44	**91** *(DL-F)*, **615**
LA206	Nov.44	**91, 122, 41**
LA207	Nov.44	**91, 1** *(JX-G)*
LA208	Nov.44	**91, 615** *(RAV-F)*
LA209	Nov.44	**91** *(DL-Q)*, **41**
LA210	Nov.44	**91** *(DL-X)*, **1, 122, 41** *(EB-X)*
LA211	May.45	**1, 122, 602**
LA212	Dec.44	**91** *(DL-F)*, **1, 122**
LA213	Jan.50	-

LA213 made its first flight in December 1944 but was modified in January 1945 by the installation of a two three blade Rotol contra-rotating propeller. After years of trials, it was eventually delivered to the RAF in January 1950 but was never issued to any unit. It was sold for scrap in July 1954.

LA214	Oct.46	**615**
LA215	Mar.45	**91**, *(DL-T)*, **615** *(RAV-A)*
LA216	Jan.47	**615**
LA217	Jan.45	**41** *(EB-?)*, **615** *(RAV-J)*
LA218	-	-
LA219	Jul.45	**1** *(JX-3)*
LA220	Jun.45	**1** *(JX-2)*
LA221	Feb.45	**91** *(DL-L)*
LA222	Jan.45	**91**, **602** *(RAI-M)*
LA223	Feb.45	**91** *(DL-Y)*, **600** *(RAG-L)*
LA224	Feb.45	**91** *(DL-V & Y)*
LA225	Feb.45	**91, 1, 122, 41** *(EB-N)*, **602**
LA226	Feb.45	**91** *(DL-E & V)*, **122**
LA227	Feb.45	**91, 602** *(RAI-O)*
LA228	Feb.45	**91, 600** *(RAG-N)*
LA229	Feb.45	**91**
LA230	Feb.45	**91**
LA231	Feb.45	**1** *(JX-M)*, **600**
LA232	Feb.45	-
LA233	Apr.45	-
LA234	Feb.45	**91** *(DL-J)*
LA235	Feb.45	**91** *(DL-T)*
LA236	Feb.45	**91** *(DL-K)*, **122**
LA249	Mar.45	**91, 600** *(RAG-M)*
LA250	Mar.45	**91, 1, 602**
LA251	Mar.45	**1, 122**
LA252	Mar.45	**91** *(DL-H)*, **122, 41**
LA253	Apr.45	**600** *(RAG-K)*
LA254	Apr.45	**91, 1, 91**
LA255	Apr.45	**1** *(JX-U)*, **91**
LA256	Apr.45	-
LA257	Apr.45	-
LA258	Apr.45	-

In addition to a full complement of ordinary Spitfire F.21s, 1 Squadron flew three contra-propeller equipped aircraft including LA220/JX-2.

LA259	Apr.45	-
LA260	Apr.45	**1, 41** *(EB-V)*
LA261	Apr.45	-
LA262	Apr.45	**1** *(JX-T)*
LA263	Apr.45	-
LA264	May.45	
LA265	May.45	**91** *(DL-K)*, **602**
LA266	May.45	**91**
LA267	Jun.45	**1** *(JX-L & Q)*, **602** *(RAI-M)*
LA268	May.45	**1** *(JX-X)*, **602**
LA269	May.45	**602** *(LO-H)*
LA270	May.45	-
LA271	May.45	-
LA272	Jul.45	**41, 91**
LA273	May.45	**1, 615** *(RAV-H later V6-H)*
LA274	Jun.45	-
LA275	Jun.45	**1** *(JX-E)*, **602** *(RAI-H)*
LA276	Jun.45	**1**
LA277	Jun.45	**1**
LA278	Jun.45	**600** *(RAG-V)*, **615**
LA279	Jun.45	**91** *(DL-U)*, **1, 602**
LA280	Jun.45	-
LA281	Jun.45	-
LA282	Jun.45	**122, 41**
LA283	Jul.45	**122, 41** *(EB-?)*, **602**
LA284	Jul.45	**91, 122, 41**
LA299	Mar.46	**1** *(JX-1)*, **41, 615, 600**
LA300	Mar.46	-
LA301	Jul.45	**1**
LA302	Jul.45	**122, 41**
LA303	Jul.45	**1**
LA304	Jul.45	**122, 41**
LA305	Jul.45	-
LA306	Jul.45	**41** *(EB-C)*, **615** *(RAV-A)*
LA307	Aug.45	-
LA308	Aug.45	**1** *(JX-O)*
LA309	Aug.45	-
LA310	Aug.45	-
LA311	Aug.45	**1**
LA312	Aug.45	-
LA313	Aug.45	**615** *(RAV-B)*
LA314	Aug.45	-
LA315	Sep.45	**41** *(EB-O)*, **602** *(RAI-K)*
LA316	Aug.45	-
LA317	Aug.45	-
LA318	Sep.45	-
LA319	Sep.45	**602** *(LO-G)*
LA320	Sep.45	-
LA321	Oct.45	-
LA322	Oct.45	-
LA323	Oct.45	**600** *(RAG-H)*
LA324	Oct.45	-
LA325	Nov.45	-
LA326	Nov.45	-
LA327	Nov.45	-
LA328	Nov.45	**600** *(RAG-J)*
LA329	Nov.45	**41, 602**
LA330	Dec.45	**600** *(RAG-F)*
LA331	Dec.45	**600** *(RAG-P)*
LA332	Jan.46	-

IN MEMORIAM
Spitfire F. 21

Name	Service No	Rank	Age	Origin	Date	Serial
Elcock, Arthur Richard	RAF No. 125505	F/L	22	RAF	14.05.45	LA200
Filmore, Eric George	RAF No. 152845	F/L	*n/k*	RAF	18.02.46	LA216
Glaser, Thomas	RAF No. 188989	F/O	*n/k*	RAF	27.09.45	LA303
Kay, Geoffrey	RAF No. 182604	F/O	22	RAF	12.05.45	LA203
Reid, Robert Ivor	RAuxAF No. 91253	F/O	30	RAuxAF	31.07.47	LA211
Sutherland, Alexander	RAF No. 174225	F/O	23	RAF	08.03.46	LA251
Trill, Jack W.E.	-	-	30	*Civil*	31.07.52	LA225

Total: 7

United Kingdom: 7

Spitfire LA217 of CFE on the ground (see photo p20). *(via C. Thomas)*

Supermarine Spitfire F. 21 LA200
No. 91 (Nigeria) Squadron
Flight Lieutenant Arthur R. ELCOCK
Ludham (UK), April 1945

William Anderson Douglas
AAF No. 90896

Bill Douglas was born in Edinburgh and joined the Auxiliary Air Force before the war in April 1939 and received his commission in June. When war broke out, he was sent to flying training school before returning to No. 603 (City of Edinburgh) Squadron in March 1940. However, just before the Germans launched their offensive in May, he was posted out as a pilot in second-line units. It was not until September that he was posted to a front-line unit, joining No. 610 Squadron in the middle of the month. In February 1941, he was back with his original squadron where he made his first claim, a damaged Bf109, on 14 June. Other claims followed that month, but he was wounded in action on the 23rd and that kept him away from operations until November when he returned to fill a flight commander's position. He stayed with 603 when it was sent to Malta. During a couple of weeks there he filed ten claim reports. In July, he took command of the squadron which disbanded two weeks later. He was then given command of a new unit, No. 229 Squadron, which he led until his tour expired at the end of September. He returned to the UK for a rest and a DFC was awarded in December. He continued to instruct until August 1943 (even though he flew on operations in May 1943 for a short spell with No. 453 Squadron) and then took command of No. 611 (West Lancashire) Squadron where he made his final claims, the very last, a Bf109 destroyed, on 14 June 1944 to make a total of six confirmed victories, three probables (one shared) and seven damaged. In September, he left 611 tour expired with a Bar to his DFC. In April 1945, he returned to operations, as wing leader of the Coltishall Wing, and was discharged from the RAF in December that year.

LA253 was delivered to the RAF in April 1945 and became from its delivery until June 1945, the mount of the Coltishall Wing Leader, Wing Commander W.A. Douglas, a Battle of Malta veteran. The codes 'WAD' are believed to be yellow. *(via C. Thomas)*

Supermarine Spitfire F. 21 LA253
Coltishall Wing
Wing Commander William A. DOUGLAS
Coltishall (UK), July 1945

Supermarine Spitfire F. 21 LA201
No. 1 Squadron
Tangmere (UK), Summer 1946

Supermarine Spitfire F. 21 LA283
No. 41 Squadron
Squadron Leader Peter W. LOVELL
Wittering (UK), 1946

Supermarine Spitfire F. 21 LA328
No. 600 (City of London) Squadron, RAuxAF
Biggin Hill (UK), 1948

SQUADRONS! - The series

1	The Supermarine Spitfire Mk VI
2	The Republic Thunderbolt Mk I
3	The Supermarine Spitfire Mk V in the Far East
4	The Boeing Fortress Mk I
5	The Supermarine Spitfire Mk XII
6	The Supermarine Spitfire Mk VII
7	The Supermarine Spitfire F. 21
8	The Handley-Page Halifax Mk I
9	The Forgotten Fighters
10	The NA Mustang IV in Western Europe
11	The NA Mustang IV over the Balkans and Italy
12	The Supermarine Spitfire Mk XVI - *The British*
13	The Martin Marauder Mk I
14	The Supermarine Spitfire Mk VIII in the Southwest Pacific - *The British*
15	The Gloster Meteor F.I & F.III
16	The NA Mitchell - *The Dutch, Poles and French*
17	The Curtiss Mohawk
18	The Curtiss Kittyhawk Mk II
19	The Boulton Paul Defiant - *day and night fighter*
20	The Supermarine Spitfire Mk VIII in the Southwest Pacific - *The Australians*
21	The Boeing Fortress Mk II & Mk III
22	The Douglas Boston and Havoc - *The Australians*
23	The Republic Thunderbolt Mk II
24	The Douglas Boston and Havoc - *Night fighters*
25	The Supermarine Spitfire Mk V - *The Eagles*
26	The Hawker Hurricane - *The Canadians*
27	The Supermarine Spitfire Mk V - *The 'Bombay' squadrons*
28	The Consolidated Liberator - *The Australians*
29	The Supermarine Spitfire Mk XVI - *The Dominions*
30	The Supermarine Spitfire Mk V - *The Belgian and Dutch squadrons*
31	The Supermarine Spitfire Mk V - *The New-Zealanders*
32	The Supermarine Spitfire Mk V - *The Norwegians*
33	The Brewster Buffalo
34	The Supermarine Spitfire Mk II - *The Foreign squadrons*
35	The Martin Marauder Mk II
36	The Supermarine Spitfire Mk V - *The Special Reserve squadrons*
37	The Supermarine Spitfire Mk XIV - *The Belgian and Dutch squadrons*
38	The Supermarine Spitfire Mk II - *The Rhodesian, Dominion & Eagle squadrons*
39	The Douglas Boston and Havoc - *Intruders*
40	The North American Mustang Mk III over Italy and the Balkans (Pt-1)
41	The Bristol Brigand
42	The Supermarine Spitfire Mk V - *The Australians*
43	The Hawker Typhoon - *The Rhodesian squadrons*
44	The Supermarine Spitfire F.22 & F.24
45	The Supermarine Spitfire Mk IX - *The Belgian and Dutch squadrons*
46	The North American & CAC Mustang - *The RAAF*
47	The Westland Whirlwind
48	The Supermarine Spitfire Mk XIV - *The British squadrons*
49	The Supermarine Spitfire Mk I - *The beginning (the Auxiliary squadrons)*
50	The Hawker Tempest Mk V - *The New Zealanders*
51	The Last of the Long-Range Biplane Flying Boats
52	The Supermarine Spitfire Mk IX - *The Former Canadian Homefront squadrons*
53	The Hawker Hurricane Mk I & Mk II - *The Eagle squadrons*
54	The Hawker biplane fighters
55	The Supermarine Spitfire Mk IX - *The Auxiliary squadrons*
56	The Hawker Typhoon - *The Canadian squadrons*
57	The Douglas SBD - *New Zealand and France*
58	The Forgotten Patrol Seaplanes
59	The Dutch Fighter Squadrons - *Nos. 322 & 120 (NEI) Squadrons*
60	The Supermarine Spitfire - *The Australian Squadrons in Western Europe and the Med*
61	The Belgian Fighter Squadrons - *Nos. 349 & 350 Squadrons*

Introducing's RAF In Combat and Bravo Bravo Aviation's collection of highly-detailed and historically accurate, high-quality aviation prints.
For more information on available prints, please visit:

 or

Prints available for this book:

PL-007: W.A. Douglas
PL-129: I.P.J. Maskill

www.ingramcontent.com/pod-product-compliance
Lightning Source LLC
Chambersburg PA
CBHW060824090426
42738CB00002B/95